Monday — Pit buckets oot on
Sunday night
   Washin' Day — Steamie at 10 am
Tuesday — Pit Waste Paper bundle
  oot
Oor turn tae dae the landin', bell
  brasses an' banisters (3rd
    Tuesday of month)
    (The meenister sometimes comes
    on a Tuesday)
Wednesday —
  Kleeneasy Man (last Wednesday)
  Rag an' Bone Man (every 6th)
  (Slimmin' class wi' Daphne) ha ha
Thursday — Wendae Cleaner for the
  outsides (last o' the month)
  Bingo Night
Friday — Pittenweem Fish Van
  Onion Johnny
    Pay the milk and the papers

Braw ⟶
butteries

VintageBakery
finest pastries since 1956

Maw Broon's Kitchen Notebook

Waverley Books

Maw's at her happiest in her kitchen makin' grub for the Broon family.

Essential Bits an' Pieces; Handy Tips an' Notes

A pinny-pocket notebook
for my favourite
kitchen secrets

Soup and Stock

Guid stock makes guid soup. Soup ingredients are like Granpaw —you need tae coax the natural sweetness oot o' them!

Don't just throw chopped vegetables into some water; fry them slowly in a soup-pot with the lid on before adding the liquid.

Making a Good Stock

* To make <u>meat stock</u> — roast the bones in some oil in the oven. Roast with vegetables such as carrots and onions. Then add everything (bits as well) to the broth pot along with water, salt and pepper, and herbs and spices.
(A 1¼ lb / 500 g hough will need about 6 pints / 3 litres of water.)
* Bring to the boil, then simmer for around four hours. <u>Stock should not be boiled or it will be cloudy.</u> Strain and chill immediately.
* Good meat stock should set like jelly. Scrape the fat from the top once chilled before using.
* <u>Ham stock</u> made from ham hough will be salty and will not need more salt added. To avoid

Making a ~~Like~~ Good Stock

an overly-salty stock, soak the
hough in cold water overnight
and discard that water before
simmering for three hours.

* To make brown vegetable stock,
roast or fry the veg first till
brown. Simmer with water,
seasoning, herbs and spices for one
hour. Season ●to taste.

* Stock or soup should be cooled
quickly after cooking and before
storing. Divide into smaller
containers and set in a basin of
iced or very cold water. Change
the water two or three times.
When cold, refrigerate or freeze.

* Stock will keep for three days
in the fridge and must be
thoroughly reheated again before
using for soup.

'THRIFTY COOK'S' SOUP TIPS

- To save time, ready-prepared broth or bouillon can be used instead of homemade. Any of the following can be a good base for a quick soup (adding extra meat, vegetables or pasta as you like): tomato, cream of chicken or mushroom tinned soups; tinned tomatoes or tomato juice; commercial stock cubes or concentrates.

- Fresh vegetables are best but some canned or frozen vegetables will work well, e.g., frozen peas, tinned or frozen sweetcorn or green beans.

- Cold soups should be served in chilled dishes.

- To reduce the fat content, make your soup the day before, chill and scrape off the fat that rises to the top. If you don't have time to chill the soup, use an unprinted paper towel to soak any oil from the surface.

- If your hot soup ends up too salty, add a whole peeled potato to the soup and simmer for approx 15 minutes to absorb some of the salt. Remove potato and serve. (The cook gets first refusal on the potato!)

- Soups always taste better if made a day or two in advance and reheated just before serving.

- Check seasonings just before serving, particularly in cold soups as chilled foods tend to dull the taste buds and will need more seasoning than hot.

- The secret of a good soup is to season it properly.

- Freeze soup in serving-size containers, ready as needed.

- You can add a little garlic to most soups to enhance the flavour – just don't overdo it!

- Use single cream instead of double to make cream soup – just as good and less than half the fat.

- Treat soup recipes as a guide – use your imagination and add your own ingredients too.

- Precook your pasta before adding to the soup. That way it doesn't bring all the starch with it and it can be added last so that it doesn't get overcooked. Use leftover pasta.

- Add fresh chopped parsley and/or coriander in the last few minutes of cooking for a wonderful fresh flavour.

Notes

Notes

Carrot and Butterbean Soup

Housewife Weekly
"cut out and keep"
Scottish Recipes

cut here ✂

1 lb / 400 g carrots, chopped
½ lb / 200 g potatoes, chopped
½ lb / 200 g butterbeans, soaked overnight
1 onion, chopped
2 pints / 1 litre vegetable stock
2 tablespoons tomato purée
Seasoning and chopped parsley

No.82

Put all ingredients in a pan and simmer for 30 mins
Blend and serve garnished with chopped parsley.

Celery — even if you dinna like the taste of it raw — is an essential ingredient when making any stock. celery is essentially boggin

I got telt that you burn mair calories eating celery than are in it!

Notes

Notes

Chicken and Sweetcorn Soup

1 lb / 400 g frozen or tinned
   sweetcorn (or fresh corn, cut from
   the cob)
1 green pepper, seeded and chopped
2 onions, chopped
2 pints / 1 litre chicken stock
1 tablespoon lemon juice
2 drops Tabasco
1 tablespoon Worcester sauce
1/2 pint / 250 ml milk
Seasoning

Put all ingredients, except the
milk, into a pan.
   Bring to the boil and simmer
30 mins.
   Blend, add milk and reheat.
   Taste for seasoning.

Sweetcorn is nae guid for Granpaw, he gets it
   stuck in his wallies

Pea and Ham Soup

2 small onions
1 clove garlic, crushed
1/2 lb / 200 g split peas, soaked
    overnight
2 1/2 pints / 1.25 litres ham stock
Seasoning
Single cream

Sauté onions and garlic.
    Add peas and stock.
    Bring to the boil, simmer 30
mins.
    Liquidise and add cream before
serving.

Use any leftover peas for your shooter

Notes

Notes

To Thicken Soup

* Remove some of the cooked vegetables from the soup, purée and return to the pot. Add extra vegetables at the beginning if you are going to do this.

* Add cream.

* Make a flour paste and blend into the soup.

* Use a roux of flour and butter and blend with the soup.

* Breadcrumbs can be added, the crumbs just disappear in the soup — a good way of using up leftover bread. (I keep a bag of breadcrumbs in the freezer.)

* Add grated raw potato and cook until soup is thickened. Or add leftover mashed potatoes.

We don't hae a lot o' leftovers at 10 Glebe Street; there's that many o' us

- Choose lean meat and reduced-fat dairy products to help minimise hidden fats.
- Use olive oil instead of butter or lard when cooking (reduces the use of saturated fats).
- Steam, bake, grill, boil or microwave your foods.
- Use non-stick cookware to eliminate the need for lubricants.
- Remove chicken skin – very high in fat.

Granpaw loves crispy chicken skin, dinna throw his away or he'll be beilin' mad. Me and Joe tae!

Meat and Fish

Recipes and cooking tips for poultry, red meat and wee fishies.

Chicken

Steep chicken pieces in milk for 30 minutes before use to stop them shrinking during cooking.

When defrosting frozen poultry (or other meat), put in a colander on top of a plate and it will defrost more quickly.

Allow hot roast poultry to ~~Leave~~ stand, covered, in a warm place for 10 minutes before carving.

After flouring uncooked chicken, chill for one hour. The coating will stick better during cooking.

Chicken meat should be cooled very quickly, preferably in a container placed in an ice-water bath. Cooked

Chicken

chicken should be stored in the refrigerator for no longer than 3–4 days.

A cooked chicken easily makes more than one meal!

Roast Chicken Dinner

To roast your chicken – rub all over with vegetable oil and season with sea salt and black pepper. As a guide, chicken should be roasted at 200°C/400°F/Gas 6 for 35–45 mins per kilo, 15–20 mins per lb.

Chicken must be cooked thoroughly! Push a skewer through the thickest part of the bird. When withdrawn, the juices must run clear.

When using a meat thermometer, the internal breast temperature must reach 165°C/330°F.

Serve with boiled or roast potatoes and vegetables of your choice.

Chill the remains of the chicken and then remove the remaining meat which can be used for salad (use breast meat), sandwiches, risottos etc.

Chicken

Don't throw out the carcass — make chicken stock! Here's a quick recipe:—

Chicken Stock
The skin and bones of a 3-lb chicken
2 carrots
1 onion
2 –3 stalks celery
1 bay leaf
1 pinch of thyme
6 peppercorns
2 pints / 1 litre water.

Break up the carcass and chop vegetables.
   Put all ingredients into a pan and bring to the boil. Simmer for 1 hour.
   Keep well skimmed.
   Strain and refrigerate until ready for use, or chill rapidly and freeze.

You can also make good stock from packets of supermarket chicken wings. Roast them first to improve the flavour.

Notes

Chicken

Chicken and Mushroom Risotto

1 large onion, chopped
1 red chilli, chopped
9 oz / 225 g mushrooms, sliced
2 tablespoons olive oil
2 oz / 50 g butter (or a bit more)
4 oz / 100 g Arborio rice
About 1 ½ pints / 800 ml chicken stock
10 oz / 250 g cooked chicken pieces
2 oz /50 g Parmesan cheese, grated
Parsley and/or coriander, chopped

1. Sauté onion, chilli and mushrooms in oil and half the butter.
2. Add the Arborio rice and fry for a few minutes without browning.
3. Add stock gradually, stirring constantly.
4. Add cooked chicken pieces 5 minutes before the end of cooking.
5. Add the rest of the butter.
6. Add the parmesan.
7. Add chopped fresh parsley and/or coriander just before serving.

(Risotto should have the consistency of porridge and the rice grains should be tender but firm.)

Easy chicken marinade:— Dash of Worcester sauce, 1 tsp mustard, juice of half a lemon and some chopped parsley. Marinade for 15 minutes and roast or fry as normal

Arborio rice is one of the classic risotto rices. Others are Carnaroli, Vialone and Baldo.

baldo is WHAT PAW is

Notes

If ye hae a real disaster wi' a burnt pot, make up a solution o' biological washing powder tae a porridge consistency and leave it overnight. It 'eats' a' the wee burnt bits.

Notes

To remove stubborn stains on crockery or bathroom tiles, make a paste of water and bicarbonate of soda and rub on with a damp cloth.

Notes

Roast Leg of Lamb

Rub the skin with oil, stab holes in the fat with the point of a knife and push sprigs of fresh rosemary and cloves of garlic into them.

Season liberally with black pepper and herb pepper.

Leave 4–5 hours or overnight.

Put some oil in a large roasting tin, brown meat to seal.

Remove meat and put vegetables for roasting in the tin then put a rack or wire tray on top.

Put the meat on the rack and place in a hot oven, 230°C / 450°F / Gas 8, for 20 minutes.

Lower heat to 180°C / 350°F / Gas 4 for remainder of the cooking time.

Roasting times may vary according to your oven.

Notes

Pork

For good crackling: Score the skin (cuts close together). Rub salt well into the scored skin. Leave overnight, wipe off and rub skin with cooking oil before putting in the oven.

Baste roast pork with cider or pineapple juice for a lovely flavour.

COOKING TEMPERATURES FOR BEEF, LAMB AND PORK

230°C / 450°F / Gas 8 for first 20 minutes. Reduce to 180°C / 350°F / Gas 4 for remainder of cooking time.

Beef and Lamb
Rare: 12–15 minutes per lb/450 g (Lamb should not be bloody, but nicely pink, so medium, below, is best)
Medium: 15 –18 minutes per lb / 450 g
Well done: 18 –20 minutes per lb /450 g
These times include the 20 minutes in the hot oven.

Pork
30 minutes per lb and 30 minutes extra at the same temperature as for beef and lamb.

Notes

Pot Roasted Beef
(serves 4)

2 ½ lbs / 1 kg topside of beef
2 teaspoons cooking oil
2 oz / 50 g butter
1 onion, chopped
2 carrots, sliced
2 stalks celery, chopped
1 large tomato, skinned and chopped
11 fl oz / 300 ml stock or water
1 wine glass red wine (optional)
Seasoning
12 small onions or shallots, peeled, whole

- Brown joint briskly in hot oil and butter (large saucepan or flameproof casserole).
- When thoroughly brown, transfer to a plate.
- Add onion, carrots and celery to pan and fry gently until golden brown.
- Replace beef, add tomatoes, stock or water, wine if used and seasoning.
- Bring to the boil. Lower heat.
- Cover pan tightly.
- Simmer very gently for 1 hour, turning at least twice.
- Add whole shallots.
- Continue to simmer further 45 mins to 1 hour (or until meat is tender).
- Serve with vegetables from the pan.

Notes

Beef Mince

(Granpaw's) Mince and Tatties

The staple of any Scottish family
— it has kept the Broons going for
years.

This is Granpaw's ain way of
cooking it — superior tae mine he
says! Hmph!

For 4 servings:—
1 onion, chopped
1 lb / 400 g lean steak mince
Carrot and turnip, diced
Seasoning
Water or beef stock

Fry the onion till soft. Add the
mince. Cook till brown.

Add enough water or beef stock to just cover the mince. Add seasoning.

Add the vegetables if liked. Season and simmer for 1 hour.

Top up with water if necessary.

To thicken, add a tablespoonful of flour blended with a little water.

Add gravy browning for added colour.

Serve up with mashed floury tatties.

FLOWERY POTAYTOES ARE FOR JESSIES

Add a tin of lentils to fresh mince to stretch it out and add to the flavour

Notes

Notes

Fish

* If fish smells 'fishy' – then it's not fresh.

* The eyes of the freshest fish should be clear.

* Flesh should be firm and a good healthy colour

Fish Cakes

250 g smoked fish, cooked
250 g cooked floury potatoes
25 g melted butter
Salt and pepper
1 egg, beaten
A little oil for frying
Dried breadcrumbs

Remove skin and bone from fish if it hasn't already been done.

Mash cooked potato, and, with a fork, mix it with the fish. Add seasoning and melted butter and mix well.

Form into four cakes. Dip in beaten egg and then coat in breadcrumbs. Fry in a frying pan in hot oil for 3 to 5 minutes each side until golden brown.

Drain on kitchen roll.

Serve immediately.

Eat up your fishy like a good boy and you'll get sponge and custard!

Poached Haddock

A guid dish if ye've been poorly —
nice and light.

2 fillets of white fish
5 fl oz / 150 ml milk
Generous knob of butter
1 tablespoon flour
Salt and pepper
1 tablespoon chopped parsley (optional)

Heat the fish in the milk and
butter till tender. Remove fish to
another plate. Blend flour with a
little of the cooking liquid. Add to
the rest of the cooking liquid and
make into a paste. Add chopped
parsley if you wish. Serve with
mashed potatoes.

Fish

Eat fish twice a week. Once should be oily fish like salmon or mackerel.

...or trout

OLD TROUT

Notes

Hen's an awfy slitter. His heid is
so far fae the plate that he's aye
dropping stuff aff his spoon on the
journey tae his mooth.

Joe - being a wee smout - disnae hae such trouble.

Notes

Just Vegetables

Ve peas a chance

Oor Maggie is occasionally vegetarian depending on who her current boyfriend is. That vegan ane wis a nice boy but a richt nuisance at tea time.

lown wi SPROUTS

As ye ken, I refuse tae go making separate dinners for a'body but we a' love oor veg. So a good veggie dinner is no great hardship tae mak' for a'body.

nae COOReiTTes heRe

Paw and Granpaw mump if they dinnae get real meat, but any o' these dishes would mah' a richt guid side dish.

Vegetable Lasagne

Replace the mince with finely chopped fried mushrooms. Quorn mince is quite nice and can be cooked the same way as beef mince. My Joe can tell the difference though.

Vegetable Stew

Make with stock or gravy and use onion, celery, aubergine, courgette, red and green peppers and tomatoes. Fry them a little first to add flavour and add herbs and spices. Season well. A tablespoon of tomato purée and a little garlic will add flavour to the gravy.

Vegetable Casserole

Make in the normal way in a casserole dish in the oven. Root vegetables like carrots, turnip and tatties are good for casseroles — add stock or gravy, onions, and mushrooms. Season well and add the herbs and spices that you like.

To thicken sauces, why not use cornflour or potato flour instead of wheat flour. Less fattening than making a white sauce with butter and flour.

Snap, rather than cut, asparagus. Each spear will naturally break where it becomes tender.

Vegetable Flan or Quiche

Pastry:
9 oz / 225 g plain flour
Pinch salt
4 oz /100 g butter, chopped into pieces
4–5 tablespoons cold water

Filling:
9 oz / 225 g mixed roast vegetables
4 oz / 100 g cheddar cheese
2 eggs, beaten
5 tablespoons milk
¼ pint /140 ml single cream
Seasoning
1 oz / 25 g cornflakes, crushed
1 tomato, sliced

1. Preheat oven to 200°C.
2. Sift flour and salt into a bowl, add butter pieces and rub into flour until it resembles fine breadcrumbs.
3. Add water and mix to a dough using a fork.
4. Knead lightly on a floured worktop.
5. Roll out pastry to line an 8-inch flan dish.
6. Prick base and bake blind at 200°C/400°F/ Gas 6 for about 10 minutes till pastry starts to colour. Remove from oven.
7. Fill flan case with roast vegetables and cheese.
8. Beat eggs, milk and cream together, add seasoning and pour into flan case.
9. Sprinkle on crushed cornflakes and bake for about 25 minutes at 200°C/ 400°F/ Gas 6.

As an addition to the beaten-egg filling you could use a can of tuna, chopped tomato, courgette, broccoli, smoked salmon, asparagus or a combination, depending on who is coming to tea! The pastry can also be adapted, e.g. add grated cheese to make cheese pastry.
Spices too can be added.
The pastry should enhance the filling and not the other way round.

Tips: When making pastry ...

- Keep ingredients as cold as possible.
- Work quickly.
- If your hands get too warm, run them under cold water to cool.
- Handle pastry little and lightly (if you don't it will be tough).
- Don't use too much extra flour when rolling out.
- When rolling pastry do not stretch it with the rolling pin – it will only spring back when cooking.
- Use 'baking beans' when baking pastry blind, to keep pastry flat and support sides.

A big Portobello mushroom fried in butter is as guid as steak!

Notes

Notes

Wrap cheese in tin foil rather than the plastic wrapping it comes in to keep it very fresh.

Cauliflower

Cooking with Vegetables

Cauliflower Crunch

1 large cauliflower, cut into sprigs
4 oz / 100 g mushrooms sliced
1 onion sliced
2 oz / 50 g butter
1 oz /25 g flour
¼ pint/ 140 ml milk
1 x 125 g carton natural yogurt
Seasoning
100 g cheddar cheese, grated
2 eggs, hard boiled and chopped
1 oz / 25 g breadcrumbs

Horace's brain

Cook the cauliflower in boiling salted water for 5 –10 minutes.

Fry onion and mushrooms in half the butter until soft.

Make a white sauce with remaining butter, and flour and milk, blend in yoghurt, seasoning and half of the grated cheese.

Place cauliflower in the base of a casserole dish, add eggs, onion and mushroom mixture on top then coat with white sauce. Mix remaining cheese with breadcrumbs and sprinkle over cauliflower. Dot with butter and brown in oven – 180°C / 350°F / Gas 4 for 10–15 mins.

We wood RATheR Take a showeR
Than eat callilfloweR

Lifestyle – Healthy Eating

- Eat lots of vegetables – they're good for you and low in calories (mostly).
- If you need to use oil, apply it with a pastry brush, or use a (brand new) plant-spray bottle filled with your favourite oil or dressing to baste or dress vegetables with a quick skoosh!
- Substitute 0%-fat Greek yoghurt for cream (just remember it can't be boiled like cream so add at the end of cooking time).
- Taste your food before adding salt.
- Add herbs for flavouring but only in the last few minutes of cooking.
- Dried herbs are stronger than fresh herbs.

You will enjoy your meal more if it looks good – spend time on presentation!

Microwave or steam your vegetables instead of boiling them — otherwise a' the goodness goes down the sink with the boiling water!

Scrub vegetables rather than peel them — many nutrients are just under the skin.

Stir-fry your vegetables in vegetable oils to preserve the vitamins. Sesame oil adds flavour to stir fries, use it sparingly at the end of the cooking time

Notes

Vegetable Garnishes

Try something different, the next time you want to decorate a plate of food. Forget the usual sprigs of greenery and wedges of tomato and try your hand at making something a little more artistic.

Carrot Curls

CARROT CURLS ARE FOR GIRLS

Peel, top and tail a carrot. Then, using a vegetable peeler, cut paper-thin strips lengthways from the carrot.

Roll up the strips and secure with a cocktail stick, place in ice water to chill thoroughly.

Remove, drain well.

Remove toothpick before using.

Carrot Flowers

To make carrot flower garnishes:

Peel carrot with vegetable peeler; place on cutting board. Cut off ends and discard. Cut carrot in half crosswise. Cut out a thin, shallow lengthwise wedge from side of carrot. Lift out wedge with tip of knife; discard wedge.

Give carrot a quarter turn. Cut out another wedge, as directed previously. Repeat, turning and cutting two more times.

Cut carrot halves crosswise into ¼-inch thick slices.

Sprinkle chopped capers onto the centre of each carrot flower. Use chives or thin strips of green onion tops for stems and parsley sprigs for leaves.

Other vegetables good for using as garnish art are cucumber, radish, courgette, peppers, tomato skins, lemon, orange, lime peel.

Cider vinegar is a lovely salad dressing, a tonic for the liver, and it's also great on brown paper, or a dry cloth, to get a shine on glass for windows!

Notes

Using Up Leftover Mashed Potatoes

Fill patty tins with mashed potato to make individual portions. Open freeze, then transfer to a polythene bag and use as required.

Make Potato Scones
9 oz / 225g leftover mashed potato
1 tablespoon butter
2 oz / 50g plain flour
3 dessertspoons milk

Beat melted butter into cold potatoes, add milk and flour and mix until smooth.

Divide into four equal pieces. Roll each out thinly, divide into four quarters and cook on a hot girdle for 2 1/2 mins each side. Cool in a clean tea towel.

Notes

Eggs

I cannae dae withoot eggs.
They are the perfect quick
meal — like a wee bit o'
French toast or an omelette
for lunch or supper. An'
bakers need them ... well ...
for nearly everything!
Mind an' buy free-range
eggs frae happy chookies!
Happy eggs taste better.

Boiled Eggs

Don't add your eggs to boiling water, the shock will crack the shells. Instead, put them into a pan (no' over big!) cover with cold water, add a pinch of salt, place pan on the hob and bring <u>slowly</u> to the boil.

From the time the water starts to simmer, 3—4 minutes will give you a really soft—boiled yolk and set white.

7 minutes will give you a firm yolk, and 10 minutes will give you a hard—boiled egg. Plunge into cold water to stop it cooking further and to stop the yolk going black.

Eggs should be simmered, not boiled, so that the white does not go tough

Poached Eggs

Forget a' the other tips for perfect poached eggs, this is the easiest one.

Line a cup with clingfilm (<u>the kind that is suitable for cooking with and microwaving</u>) and crack an egg into the clingfilm.
There should be enough clingfilm to allow you to tie it around the top of the egg.

Drop the egg into boiling water and poach normally.
A nice shape, no slittery white bits and the pan is easily cleaned!

The Broons' But an' Ben Biled Egg Chart:
An Exercise Requiring Military Precision

Granpaw	2 eggs	very soft	3 mins
Paw	2 eggs	very soft	3 mins
Maw	1 egg	soft	4 mins
Maggie	1 egg	soft	4 mins
Daphne	3 eggs	soft	4 mins
Hen	2 eggs	soft	4 mins
Joe	2 eggs	hard	7 mins
Horace	1 egg	hard	7 mins
Ae Twin	1 egg	hard	7 mins
Ither Twin	1 egg	hard	7 mins
Bairn	1 egg	hard	10 mins
	_____	(chapped up	
	17 eggs	in a cup wi'	
		butter)	

Start wi' 17 eggs in cold water. Eggs should
be simmered not boiled. Heat slowly. Time it
from when the water starts tae simmer. Pit
the toast on.

Pit 12 bits o' bread on tae toast.
6 sojers per slice o' toast.
4 toast sojers for 17 eggs = 68 sojers
= 12 bits o' toast (wi' fower extra sojers
for whoever gets tae them the quickest).

Efter 3 minutes, tak' oot 4. Efter 4 minutes
tak oot 7. By the time you've doled those
oot wi' buttered toast sojers, it'll be time
tae get the rest oot an served up.

Shell the Bairn's egg. Put in an old mug wi'
a dod o' butter an' chap it up wi' a knife.
She eats it wi' a wee spoon.

Very fresh eggs take aboot a minute
longer tae boil than auld anes

Egg Tips

Take eggs out of the fridge 30 minutes before cooking to allow them to reach room temperature.

Use a non-stick pan for scrambled eggs or omelettes.

When frying eggs, spoon the hot oil over the egg yolk to speed up cooking.

Always serve an omelette on a warm plate.

When whisking egg whites make sure the bowl is grease free by rinsing it in boiling water before starting and drying thoroughly. Any grease, soap, or yolk in the bowl will prevent the egg whites from whisking up.

When baking with several eggs in one recipe, crack each one into a separate dish before adding it to the mixture. This gives you the chance to avoid accidentally adding a stale egg or bits of shell into the mix.

If you are not good at separating eggs: crack the egg onto a plate. Place a cup over the yolk and pour the white into a bowl.

Is that egg fresh?

YOU CAN test an egg to see if it's fresh, without cracking it, by putting it in a bowl of water. A stale egg will float and a fresh egg will sink. This is because as an egg gets older some liquid evaporates from the egg through its porous shell. The egg starts to weigh less than the amount of water it displaces and so it floats. Older eggs are best for hard boiling and baking. Stale eggs should be discarded!

Once cracked open, odour and appearance will immediately tell you if an egg is stale!

Lifestyle – Diets

- Crash diets and starving yourself don't work – you need to eat properly to lose weight healthily longterm!
- Eat slowly and savour every mouthful.
- Enjoy your food, it should be a pleasure not a chore.
- And last but not least ... Everything in moderation!

Notes

Notes

The perfect accompaniment tae a wee cake … is a guid strong cup o' tea! To mak' the best tea, use real tea leaves — no' tea bags! Granpaw says teabags are fu' o' dust! Assam loose tea is his favourite.

The water must be biling when it hits the leaves, or the tea will be insipid. Warm the teapot before you start.

Despite what Paw Broon might think, drinking hot tea oot yer saucer tae cool it doon is no' guid manners. And wafting it wi' yer bunnet is no' much better, Granpaw.

Cakes, Pastry and Baking

Maist folk hae got mair baking
recipes in their cookery notebooks
than a' the ithers — and I'm nae
   different.
We a' love a wee cake — though the
   way tae Paw's heart wis — and
still is — wi' a guid plate o' mince
   an' tatties!

PASTRY

How much pastry do you need to line a tart tin?

Subtract 2 inches from the diameter to find the amount of flour, in ounces, that you need.

You will need half that amount in butter.

For example:

For an 8-inch tin you will need 6 oz flour and 3 oz butter.

Pastry tips

Pastry ingredients should be chilled, but make sure the butter is soft enough to rub in.

Sift the flour well before rubbing in the butter.

Too much liquid will make the pastry tough and hard to roll, too little and it will be crumbly and fall apart.

Handle the pastry as little as possible when making and rolling out to avoid making it tough.

For short pastry, when rubbing in, use the fingertips and lift them into the air, this allows air to get into the pastry and makes it lighter and more delicate.

Chill, or rest, the pastry in the fridge for at least 30 minutes after making. Do so again after rolling to avoid shrinking.

Shape your pastry before chilling – it makes rolling it out easier.

Place tart tins on a preheated oven tray in the oven to crisp the base.

Notes

Notes

Bread

Plain White Bread

Makes 2 x 1-lb loaves

1½ lbs /675 g strong white flour
1 teaspoon salt
1 oz / 25 g lard
1 sachet easy blend dried yeast
1 teaspoon caster sugar
16 fl oz / 450 ml warm water.

Sift flour and salt into a warm mixing bowl and rub in lard. Add yeast and mix well, then stir in warm water.

Stir and mix until the dough starts to form. Knead first in the bowl and then on a lightly floured surface until you have a soft, elastic dough. Put the dough into a clean, lightly greased bowl, cover and set aside in a warm place to rise until almost double in size (about 30–40 mins).

Grease two 1-lb loaf tins. Knock back the risen dough, divide it into two pieces and shape to fit loaf tins. Press the dough into the tins, cover and leave to prove for a further 10–15 mins, or until the dough is just above the top of the tins.

Bake in a hot oven, Gas 8/230°C/450°F for about 30–40 minutes until brown. Turn out and cool on a wire tray.

Keeps fresh for 3–4 days, or freezes for up to 1 month.

Some bread tips

Raw bread dough freezes well. After kneading, form the dough into a ball and place in a large lightly greased polythene bag. Seal very tightly, label and freeze. Use plain white within 1 month.

Ensure cooked bread is completely cold before freezing.

Slice the bread before freezing allowing individual slices to be removed for use without defrosting the whole loaf.

Glazes for bread

Soft crust glaze – brush with oil or dust with flour. For a really brown soft crust – brush with a milk and sugar mixture.

Shiny brown crust – brush with beaten egg.

Shiny finish only – brush with egg white.

Crisp crust – brush with salt water glaze. Dissolve 1 teaspoon salt in 2 tablespoons water.

Sweet glaze – Stir 1 tablespoon water and a little sugar into a beaten egg and brush over the dough.

Honey glaze – Stir 1 tablespoon runny honey into 2 tablespoons water and brush over the dough.

The Cake Recipe You Can Adapt to Make Any Cake

This is my lovely and adaptable Madeira Cake

For an 8-inch round tin:

7 oz / 175 g plain flour
7 oz / 175 g self-raising flour
11 oz / 275 g butter or soft cake margarine
11 oz / 275 g caster sugar
5 medium eggs (beaten)
3 tablespoons milk.
1 teaspoon vanilla flavouring

Prepat the oven to 180°C / 350°F / Gas 4

Cream butter and sugar together.

Sift together flours.

Beat together eggs, milk and vanilla flavouring.

Gradually add egg mixture and flours alternately to creamed margarine and sugar. Mix well until blended.

Turn into a lined cake tin and cook on the middle shelf of the oven for about 1 1/2 — 1 3/4 hours.

When cooked, the cake should feel firm to slight pressure and spring back when slightly pressed down. If a skewer is inserted, it should come out clean and dry.

Use your favourite sponge cake recipe and replace some of the flour with cocoa powder. The more flour replaced, the stronger the flavour.

See the next page for my chocolate cake recipe. p. t. o.

Chocolate Cake

Always add a teaspoonful of vanilla flavouring to a chocolate cake.

I use my Madeira cake recipe and replace some of the plain flour with cocoa powder.

For a chocolate cake replace:—
3 oz / 75 g of the plain flour with 3 oz / 75 g of cocoa powder.
If you prefer a lighter chocolate flavour use drinking chocolate powder.

QUICK TIPS

To stop a mixing bowl spinning round as you mix cakes or meringues, place a damp tea towel undearneath it.

Make Any Cake

The basic sponge cake recipe can be used for:

Cherry Cake — add 8 oz / 200 g halved glace cherries

Coconut Cake — add 3 oz / 75 g dessicated coconut

Nut Cake — replace 5 oz / 125 g plain flour with 5 oz / 125 g ground nuts of your choice.

Citrus Cake — add the grated rind and juice of 2 lemons, oranges or limes.

Madeira Cake is very versatile and can be used instead of fruit cake at Christmas or for wedding cakes.

To ice — omit marzipan, cover with a very thin layer of butter-cream icing and then cover with fondant icing as you would a fruit cake.

Cake Trouble!

Every baker has had a cake that flopped ... or cracked ... or burnt!

To prevent anything going wrong, the best tip I can give you is to read the recipe properly, and several times, before you start. So many times a recipe seemingly fails ... but often it's because something was missed out or misread.

If something goes wrong, go back to the recipe. Did you follow it to the letter? Baking is even more of a science than it is an art! Measurements must be precise.

So if you're sure you followed the recipe, what else could have happened?

• If your cake sank:- Did you open the door of the oven before it was cooked (a large cake may need at least an hour to 'set')? Was it underbaked? Have you accidentally added too much butter?

• If your cake is domed and cracked on top:- Was the oven temperature too high. Did you add too much raising agent? Did you mix in the raising agent well enough (if you can see little 'explosions' in the cake this is a likely reason)? Is your cake tin a size too small?

• If all the fruit sank to the bottom:- Was it mixed in well enough? Was your mixture too runny? Why not also try coating the fruit in flour before adding to cake batter next time.

• If your cake was too dry:- Was the cake baked for too long at too high a temperature? Is your oven's temperature control telling the truth? Test your oven with an oven thermometer.

• If your cake is too dense and heavy:- Did you add the eggs too quickly? Did the butter and egg mix look curdled? Add flour and eggs gradually next time.

Notes

Notes

Carrot Cake

12 oz / 300 g plain flour
2 teaspoons cinnamon
1 teaspoon baking powder
½ teaspoon bicarbonate of soda
8 oz / 200 g brown sugar
4 eggs
9 fl oz / 250 ml oil
1 orange, zested
1 lemon, zested
8 oz / 200 g carrots, finely grated
6 oz / 150 g walnuts, chopped
9 oz / 227 g tin pineapple pieces, well drained, chopped (optional)

• Heat oven to 150°C/ 300°F / Gas 2. Line a 20-cm x 10-cm-deep cake tin.
• Sift dry ingredients together and stir in sugar.
• Beat eggs with oil and add zests. Stir in carrots.
• Fold egg mixture into flour mixture. Fold in walnuts and pineapple.
• Spoon into tin and bake for approximately 1 hour 20 mins or until a skewer
  comes out clean. Cool.

Cream Cheese Frosting

5 oz / 125 g unsalted butter at room temperature
2 oz / 50 g icing sugar
10 oz / 250 g cream cheese

• Beat butter and sugar together until soft and then beat in cream cheese. Chill
  until thick but still spreadable.
• Spread a thick layer on top of the cake, making sure the side of the icing is flat
  and continues upwards from the side of the cake.

Date and Walnut Loaf

225g chopped dates
A pinch bicarbonate of soda
150ml boiling water
225g self-raising flour
75g margarine
75g caster sugar
1 medium beaten egg
75g chopped walnuts
1 tsp gravy browning (if you are brave enough)!

Sprinkle bicarbonate of soda over dates in bowl and pour over boiling water. Allow to soak for 30 minutes. Rub margarine into sieved flours and add sugar, walnuts, egg and gravy browning. Lastly add the soaked date mixture. Mix thoroughly, place in a 2-lb greased loaf tin and bake Gas 4 / 180°C / 350°F for about 1 hour.

Tea Loaf

8 oz / 200 g mixed dried fruit
4 oz / 100 g soft brown sugar
4 fl oz / 125 ml warm tea
8 oz / 200 g SR flour
1 teaspoon mixed spice
1 dessertspoon marmalade
1 egg

Soak fruit and sugar in tea overnight. Sieve dry ingredients, then blend all together thoroughly. Place in a greased and floured loaf tin and bake at Gas 4 / 180°C / 350°F for about 1 hour.

Notes

Pancakes / Scones

Are longer-life pancakes what has kept Granpaw going as long?

Longer-Life Scotch Pancakes

The addition of the oil improves the
shelf life of Scotch pancakes –
they keep softer longer.

8 oz / 200 g self-raising flour
1 level teaspoon salt
1 oz / 25 g sugar
1 dessertspoon syrup
1 large egg
9 fl oz / 250 ml milk (approx)
1 dessertspoon veg oil (approx)

Sieve dry ingredients
Add egg, syrup and sufficient milk to give a thick batter consistency, add
oil and beat in.
Drop mixture in spoonfuls onto a fairly hot girdle or non-stick frying
pan.
Cook until lightly browned, turn pancake and brown second side.
Cool in a clean tea towel.

Longer-Life Scones

Add a little oil and 1 egg to make up the 125 ml milk measure per 200 g
quantity. Helps to keep the scones soft longer.

8 oz / 200 g self-raising flour
¼ teaspoon bicarbonate of soda
Pinch salt
40g / 1 ½ oz butter
Milk – or buttermilk – with egg and a little oil made up to 125 ml

Preheat oven to 190°C / 375°F / Gas 5. Sift flour and bicarbonate of
soda into a bowl. Rub in butter. Use a knife to mix in liquid to a soft
dough. Turn out on to floured surface and work quickly to cut out
rounds. Put on baking sheet on middle shelf and cook for approx 10–15
mins.

Notes

Baking

Doughnuts (without yeast)
8 oz / 200 g self-raising flour
Pinch salt
2 ½ oz / 65 g butter
2 oz / 50 g sugar
1 egg, beaten
Milk to mix
Oil (for deep-frying)

Sift dry ingredients (except the sugar).
Rub in butter with the fingertips till it resembles
breadcrumbs. Then add the sugar and mix through
thoroughly. Mix in the egg and enough milk to
make a light dough. Roll out and cut into rings.
Deep-fry in hot oil until golden brown.
Drain and toss in sugar while hot, or glaze with
icing when cool.

This maks aboot 8, so I need
to mak three batches for my
lot

Notes

Notes

Shortbread

A classic! A'body has aye got their ain version.
I cannae say I've ever had a bit of shortbread I didnae like so I dare say they are a' worth a try!

Shortbread

8 oz / 200 g plain flour
4 oz / 100 g butter
2 oz / 50 g caster sugar
More caster sugar for dredging

Mix flour and sugar. Rub flour and sugar gradually into butter, at room temperature, using the fingertips.

Knead well, shape or cut into rounds or biscuits, or spread into a tray.

Place on a baking tray, pinch edges (except biscuits), prick with a fork.

Bake at 170 –180°C / 340–350°F / Gas 3–4 for about 15 mins or until pale brown.

Remove from oven and immediately dust with caster sugar.

Cut into strips.

Allow to cool for a short time before removing from tray or moving.

Variations

Substitute 50g plain flour for 50g rice flour (crunchier texture).

Substitute 50g plain flour for 50g fine semolina.

Substitute 50g plain flour with 50g cornflour and use icing sugar instead of caster sugar (smooth texture).

Use granulated sugar instead of caster (courser texture).

Ginger Biscuits – add 1–2 oz / 25–50 g chopped crystallised ginger.

Cherry Biscuits – add 2 oz / 50 g chopped cherries.

Pitcaithly Bannocks – add 2 oz / 50 g blanched almonds and chopped citron peel.

Highlander Biscuits – roll the shortbread into a long sausage shape, roll in Demerara Sugar, wrap in greaseproof paper and chill for 30 minutes or so. Slice into 15 pieces, put on a baking tray and bake until golden brown.

The shortbread recipe can be used for Empire Biscuits too.

Banana Loaf

A great way to use up bananas afore they go aff.

```
Banana Loaf
2 oz / 50 g butter or margarine
5 oz / 125 g sugar
2 eggs
8 oz / 200 g self-raising flour
Pinch salt
2 mashed ripe bananas


Cream fat and sugar.
Beat in eggs.
Add dry ingredients and banana
alternately.
Beat until smooth.
Bake in greased and floured 1-lb loaf
tin at Gas 5 / 190°C / 375°F for
about 1 hour.
```

Notes

Meringues

Meringues will never work unless the bowl is completely dry and clean.

I whip the egg whites until they are that stiff I can hold the bowl upside down ower Paw's heid.

Agnes says:
"My recipe is 3 egg whites and 7 oz caster sugar. Bake at 50°C overnight and put in an airtight container while still warm."

Best meringues I've tasted and always the same quality!

Meringues

MERINGUES

- Bowls and equipment must be totally grease free.
- Use older egg whites. If they are very fresh add tiny pinch of salt before whisking. Allow whites to come to room temperature before whisking.
- Don't add sugar till the whites are whisked till firm.
- Any trace of yolk and the whites will not whip properly.
- Use a very clean bowl, rinse with boiling water to ensure any grease traces are removed. Allow bowl to cool before using.
- Use eggs that are over a 1 week old. Fresh egg whites do not whip so well.
- Whip the egg whites until they are so stiff and firm that the bowl can be turned upside down without them falling out. An electric whisk makes the job easy.
- Meringues can be frozen, unfilled, and packed in a box to prevent damage.
- Meringues can be baked in a very slow oven, 110°C / 212°F / Gas ¼ for 1 ½ hours. Take from the oven, carefully remove from baking parchment lining the tray, gently press a small hole in the base of each meringue with the thumb. Place them upside down on the baking tray and return them to the oven for further ¾ of an hour to 1 hour.

Puddings

The best puddings are maist likely the simplest anes. Ye need a contrast, mind — tangy, tart aipple goes wi' sweet crumbly pastry ... an' ye canny forget the smooth creamy custard. Sweet desserts like Sticky Toffee Pudding need ice-cream or a big dollop o' double cream to balance out ony sichly sweetness — as well as a guid flavouring o' allspice, cinnamon or nutmeg in the mix.

Notes

Rhubarb notes

In summer I use the But an' Ben
Rhubarb for:

Rhubarb Crumble
Rhubarb Tart
Rhubarb Pie
Rhubarb Jam
Rhubarb Chutney
Rhubarb Snow — ● made wi'
   whipped egg whites ... no' real
   snow, though we get plenty at
   the But an' Ben.
Aepples can be used instead o'
rhubarb for maist o' the above.

Can also be combined with:
Aepple ... for Chutney,
   Ginger and Apricot for braw jam.
Add ground ginger to crumble.
Add ground cloves to the jam too.

Rhubarb Pie

Shortcrust pastry (make with
8 oz / 200g flour, 4 oz / 100 g
butter)
2 lbs / 900 g chopped rhubarb
4 oz / 100 g sugar
A little cornflour

Preheat oven to 220°C / 425°F /
Gas 5. Divide pastry in half. Roll
out a base for the pie dish.
    Dust the base of the pie with a
little cornflour. Mix the fruit and
sugar and about 2 tsps cornflour
and fill the pie. (The cornflour
combines with the juice to make
a thick syrup. It also helps to stop
the pie from becoming too soggy.)

TIP: *Try using self-raising flour
instead of plain flour for the pastry
as this will help to prevent a chasm
forming between the pastry and the
fruit when baking.*
    Roll out rest of the pastry and
top the pie.
    Make a hole in the centre to let
out the steam.
    Bake for 30–40 minutes at
180°C/ 350°F/Gas 4.

*There's nae point in hacin' a
pudding withoot custard*

Custard

Custard 1

9 fl oz / 250 ml milk
2 egg yolks or 1 whole egg
2 dessertspoons sugar
Vanilla flavouring

Heat the milk and pour over the beaten eggs, strain back into the rinsed pan.
Stir continuously over a low heat until the sauce thickens but do not allow to boil. Add sugar and flavouring.

Custard 2

9 fl oz / 250 ml milk
2 level dessertspoons cornflour
1 oz / 25g sugar
1 egg
Vanilla flavouring

Measure 3 dsps milk into a bowl, add cornflour and mix well until smooth. Heat remainder of milk to below boiling point. Remove from heat and stir in cornflour mixture. Bring to the boil. Stir until thickened and simmer for 2 mins.
Remove from heat, stir in the sugar, beaten egg and vanilla flavouring.

Curdling happens when egg mixtures are cooked on too high a heat or for too long. There's a reason recipes state, "stir constantly over low temperatures".
If you have a blender, pour the curdled custard in, cover and blend until smooth, return to a clean pan and continue cooking.
Or, pass through a sieve into a cold bowl. Or, whisk in 2 tablespoons of cold double cream.

Notes

Notes

Puddings

THRIFTY COOK'S TIPS OF THE DAY ...

Today ... Desserts

Glaze fruits in a flan with a couple of melted lemon jelly cubes in a little water or with fruit juice from tinned fruit, thickened with arrowroot (for a clear glaze). If cornflour is used for thickening, a cloudy glaze will result.

Use ginger biscuits instead of sponges at the base of a trifle.

Cover trifles with a mixture of crushed meringue shells and whipped cream. Grate chocolate on top.

To increase the volume of double cream, mix two parts double cream with one part single cream.
or
When halfway through whipping 150 ml double cream, dilute with 2 tablespoons of milk or plain yoghurt for a lighter effect.

Store cartons of sour or double cream upside down in the refrigerator to keep them fresh longer.

Pipe unused whisked fresh cream into rosettes on a baking sheet and freeze for use at a later date.

Bananas will freeze successfully if you peel and slice them before placing in an airtight container.

When using banana in a fruit salad, cover the unpeeled banana with cold water for 15 mins before use. This should prevent it going black in the salad.

These tips are the berries!

Notes

Notes

Quick Black Forest Pudding

1 chocolate Swiss roll
(bought or home made)
A little sherry
Tin of black cherries
Double cream, whipped
Chocolate sprinkles

Housewife Weekly
"cut out and keep"
Scottish Recipes

cut here ✂

No.44

Slice chocolate Swiss roll and line a trifle dish, sprinkle on some sherry and some juice from a tin of black cherries. Cover with halved black cherries, whip some double cream to soft peaks and spread on. Cover with chocolate sprinkles.

Honeydew melon is high in vitamin C, but it will take on the smell of the fridge if you leave it in there cut in half, so I always slice it up and keep it in a container for the next day if we don't finish it.

Sweeties

Us Broons hae a sweet tooth (or
is that sweet teeth?). I like my
jube-jubes, Paw likes a bit o' toffee,
Granpaw likes granny sookers, and
Daphne likes a soor-ploom. It's guid
fun making yer ain sweeties though.
A good tip to stay slim would be tae
only eat sweeties that you've made
yersel — that's harder work than
just buying them oot a shop.
I dinnae ken how tae mah'
jube-jubes though.

Sweeties

General tips for sweet-making

1. When boiling sugar use a strong, thick-based pan that allows for the contents to boil up. A jelly pan is a good option.
2. Brush round the sides of the pan constantly with a pastry brush dipped in warm water to remove sugar crystals.
3. Invest in a sugar thermometer.
4. Keep the thermometer in a pan of hot water at the side of the cooker. Takes less time to reach actual temperature.
5. When testing syrup, read the thermometer in upright position, with your eye level with the top of the mercury. Make sure the mercury bulb of the thermometer is in the middle of the mixture – do not rest it on the bottom of the pan. Alternatively, use a digital thermometer.

Be very careful when you're working wi' boiling sugar!

Helensburgh Toffee

My favourite! (It's really <u>tablet!</u>)

1 lb 4 oz / 500 g granulated sugar
4 fl oz / 125 ml milk or water
2 oz / 50 g butter
1 dessertspoon golden syrup
7 fl oz / 200 ml condensed milk
Vanilla flavouring

Melt butter with water or milk.
Stir gently. Add sugar and syrup.
Stir. When dissolved, add condensed
milk. Stir all the time, boil to
118°C (soft ball). Remove from heat,
allow to settle, add flavouring.

Beat till beginning to grain;
quickly pour into a greased tin,
15—20 cm in size.

When set, cut into squares.
If you fancy making additions
to tablet then use the following

p.t.o.

Tablet

recipe (I wouldn't adulterate the Helensburgh Toffee recipe at any cost, it's too braw just as it is!)

Vanilla Tablet

Yet another version of tablet — I think I hen about five different anes! (A'body aye hens the 'best' yin so they wid have ye believe. Scunners.)

1 lb 4 oz / 500 g granulated sugar
2 oz / 50 g butter
9 fl oz / 250 ml milk
1 tablespoon golden syrup
Vanilla flavouring

1. Put sugar, butter, milk, syrup in a pan. Stir gently to dissolve sugar.

Tablet

2. Bring slowly to the boil.
3. Boil to 115°C /239°F (soft ball), stirring all the time.
4. Remove from heat, add vanilla.
5. Beat till beginning to grain.
6. Pour into greased tin (15–20 cm) and cut when cold.

Tablet Variations

Walnut Tablet — add 3 oz / 75g chopped walnuts before beating as in the basic tablet recipe.

Cherry Tablet — add 3 oz / 75g chopped glacé cherries before beating.

Pineapple Tablet — add 3 oz / 75g crushed, well-drained, pineapple before beating.

Chocolate Tablet — add 2 oz / 50g grated chocolate at step 1.

Notes

Peppermint Creams

If you don't fancy working with boiling sugary liquids (like when you're cooking with bairns) this is a good recipe.

LET'S COOK

Peppermint Creams

1 lb 4 oz / 500 g sieved icing sugar
2 egg whites
Peppermint flavouring

Slightly whisk egg whites.
Gradually stir in icing sugar till a stiff consistency is reached.
Add peppermint flavouring and knead well.
Roll out on board with icing sugar.
Cut into small rounds and leave overnight to dry on greaseproof or silicone paper.

A drop of green colouring could be added, if wished, to give the creams that cool green mint look.
If wished, the creams could be half dipped in your favourite melted chocolate and left to dry on greaseproof or silicone paper.

Notes

Truffles

Sherry Truffles

9 oz / 225 g digestive biscuits
7 fl oz / 200 ml condensed milk
1½ oz / 40 g dessicated coconut
2 oz / 50 g butter
2 oz / 50 g drinking chocolate
1 fl oz / 30 ml sherry

Crush biscuits finely (put in a polythene bag and use a rolling pin to crush). Add dry ingredients. Melt butter and milk in a pan. Pour this over the dry mixture and then add sherry. Stir.
Leave to firm in the fridge for a short time. Then roll into balls and coat with chocolate sprinkles or dessicated coconut or cocoa powder.

Instead of sherry, spiced rum, Cointreau or vanilla flavouring could be used if preferred.

*The best truffles
I have tasted!*

Jams, Jellies and Marmalades

A wee taste of summer all year round makes all the hard work of jam-making — boiling, straining, waiting, standing, stirring, getting bubbled on and splashed and altogether roasting hot! — worth all the effort.

Nothing is nicer than toast an' butter spread thick wi' home-made jam that you've just made yersel' ... and is still just a wee bit warm. Braw!

Jam Tips

Rhubarb makes great jam, is a very easy fruit to work with and stores in the freezer very well for future use.

Jellies

It's a lot easier to make some fruits into jellies than to make them into jam — even although jelly-making has three stages to it.

1. Boiling up.
2. Straining (in a jelly bag).
3. Boiling with sugar to make the jelly.

Blackcurrants, redcurrants, brambles (blackberries) and gooseberries all make great jam but are an absolute footer to prepare. So it's much easier to boil up and extract the juice by straining — no bits!

Maw with a bath tub fu' o' blackcurrant juice
— from fruit picked at Granpaw's allotment —
strained for jeely. Next time I used that
bath for steeping my good silk simmits
they went a' purple.

Crab apples make the best fruit jelly!

Marmalade Tips

Marmalade is also a right footer to make! It's in my big cookbook page 15, an' the But an' Ben Cookbook pages 113–115.

Use marmalade for things other than just spreading on your toast:

Add it to cakes as a flavouring.

An ingredient for steamed puddings.

Glaze on ham, chicken, or gammon.

Remove pith, spread thinly on top of fruit cakes to help marzipan to stick.

Sweet and sour sauce:– in a pan heat ½ cup tomato ketchup, ½ cup marmalade (no pith). And, to your own taste, add the following: soy sauce, white vinegar, sugar, water. Add a teaspoon cornflour to thicken, and heat through.

Cooking with Marjorie

MAKING MARMALADE

- Make it in small batches – so much easier and quicker.
- Use only the thin outer peel from citrus fruits, the white pith and membranes are rather bitter.
- Don't throw out the pith, membrane and seeds, tie them in a piece of muslin and cook along with the rest of the fruit. They contain pectin which is necessary for the gelling process.

- To get more juice from citrus fruit, put them in the microwave for about 10 seconds, cool and then roll in your hands using a slight pressure to break down the cells holding the juice.
- Zest is easiest removed from the whole fruit.
- Remember to wash all fruit thoroughly before using.
- Leftover zest will keep for 6 months in the freezer sealed in a polythene bag. Use straight from frozen.

Notes

Strawberry Jam

Strawberry Jam can be one of the most difficult to make because of its low pectin content (pectin is the stuff that makes jam set).

It can be made very successfully by two tried-and-tested methods.

Use **Jam Sugar** and follow the recipe on the bag. This sugar has added pectin and is especially for making jam with fruits of low pectin content like strawberries and raspberries.

Add commercial **pectin** to the strawberries instead of fruit juice as directed in some recipes. Can be purchased in some supermarkets and some high street chemists.

Making strawberry jam using only sugar produces a nice flavour but it must be made from dry fruit in good condition. It doesn't gel but is pleasantly syrupy. Makes a great topping for ice cream or as a strawberry sauce.

1 kg strawberries, washed and hulled
1 kg jam sugar

- Sterilise some jam jars. Wash in soapy water. Rinse and dry. Place upside down on a tea towel on a baking tray and place in a cool oven (100°C / 212°F / Gas ¼) till you are ready to pot the jam.
- Heat strawberries in a jelly pan till the juice flows.
- Add sugar and boil quickly for 15 minutes.
- Test on a chilled plate.
- Dribble a little jam on it.
- Allow to cool.
- Push it with your finger.
- If it wrinkles the jam is ready.
- Pot while the jam is still warm.
- Fill the jars right up to the brim and place a disc of waxed paper on the top.

Party Time

Us Broons like a do! Halloween,
Christmas, Hogmanay, Burns
Night, the bairns' (including
Granpaw's) birthdays, any excuse
for us to have a pairty.

Be prepared and it will a' be fine.
Fail to plan, then plan to fail
as someone once said! I think it
might have been my mither.

Sandwiches

A standard pan loaf has 22 slices, therefore will make 44 small square sandwiches.

Buy a crustless sandwich loaf – no waste cutting off the crusts.

Keep the fillings simple – there is nothing worse than the filling falling out of your sandwich and making a mess on your guests' clothes and the floor.

Don't use raw onion or other strong flavours in sandwiches, your guests will want to taste the other goodies on offer and it will overpower their tastebuds.

Remember, presentation is everything. Your guests will judge your food by appearance before taste!

- For sandwiches – switch to wholemeal or wholegrain bread.
- Don't butter the bread. If your fillings are tasty enough, you'll never miss it.
- Try replacing butter with a thin spread of peanut butter, other nut spreads, hummus, low fat cheese spreads or avocado.

Wine: Using 125 ml glasses you will get 6 glasses per bottle. A 3-litre box of wine will give you 24 glasses.

PLANNING A PARTY CHECKPOINTS

- Plan well in advance.
- Decide on the type of party – tea party, dinner, buffet, children's.
- List your menu – and stick to it when you go shopping.
- Make out a list of all the ingredients and then check your store cupboard.
- First make food items that can be made and frozen in advance
- Get all your disposable cutlery, plates, napkins and table covers in advance if being used (large number parties only).
- Work out a furniture plan and which rooms will be out of bounds to guests.
- Make a work plan of cooking and cleaning to be done and don't leave yourself too exhausted to enjoy yourself
- If you are offered help in preparation take it! Get two or three friends you work well with to help you.

Dinna let the boys make their famous "party punch".

Hangovers: cold tea bags can relieve itching, inflamed eyes as may occur with hayfever ... or too much wine. Slices of cucumber work well too.

The day before a party

- Get starters and puddings made.
- Organise your rooms.
- Lay tables.
- Clean.
- Food preparation for the next day.
- Get all your serving dishes looked out and washed.

The day of the party

- Always serve food on clean plates.
- Wash all fruit and vegetables.
- Warm dishes for hot food.
- Cold food on platters should be placed over bowls of ice to keep them cold.
- Don't overfill your fridge – cold air must be allowed to circulate to keep food safe.
- Replace empty food platters rather than re-fill them.
- Keep raw and cooked food separate – avoid cross contamination!
- Do not leave food at room temperature for more than 2 hours.
- Remember to have a good selection of soft drinks available. Not everyone likes to drink alcohol and remember those who have to drive home.
- Don't run out of food – have garlic or herb bread on standby.
- If you don't have enough refrigerator space for chilling drinks, fill a large plastic tub with ice and push bottles and cans into the ice – a very decorative way of keeping drinks cold.
- To chill a room-temperature can or bottle really fast – add a dessertspoon of salt to a bowl of cold water and ice, place your choice into the bowl and leave for two to three minutes (much faster than the freezer, and safer, just in case you are distracted and forget).
- To help prevent a hangover, put a few drops of juniper oil on your pillow, it is a good detoxifier. (Worth a try!)

Notes

First published 2010 by Waverley Books,
144 Port Dundas Road, Glasgow, G4 0HZ
© 2010 Waverley Books and DC Thomson & Co Ltd.

Broons cartoons and characters appear courtesy of
and are © ® 2010 DC Thomson & Co Ltd
Other elements created by Hugo Breingan.

Recipes and tips by Gilda T Smith
Layout by Hugo Breingan

Acknowledgments:
With thanks to Agnes Lamont, Auntie Kate,
Pat Small, Jim Cooper and Margaret Cowan

Photos:
Endpapers: vintage labels courtesy of Jim Cooper, with thanks to
Kenneth Sandford. Pages 28, 32, 51, 79, 84, 96, 119 and
cover background courtesy of Shutterstock. Page 82 E Abraham.

ISBN 978-1-84934-036-6

2 3 4 5 6 7 8 9 10

Printed and bound in the EU.

Glebe Street School
Bicentenary Party Committee

Security: Aggie Gow - on the door;
keep oot the gatecrashers and meet
and greet (mind and smile).

Cloakroom: Jessie - get pins and
tickets. (Dinnae get tickets the
same colour as the raffle tickets.)

Minglers: Jean, Nancy, Janice
(Stott). Make the shy folk feel at
hame and take the bare look off the
anes that are there themsels.

Welcome drinks:
Bert: get glasses frae Oddbuckets.
Theresa Murphy: trays.
Bert and Theresa to serve drinks.
... o' a bottle o' fizz per heid.
... ses o' 6 bottles. Get them
... r return fae Erchie Stott.